Paper Circuits

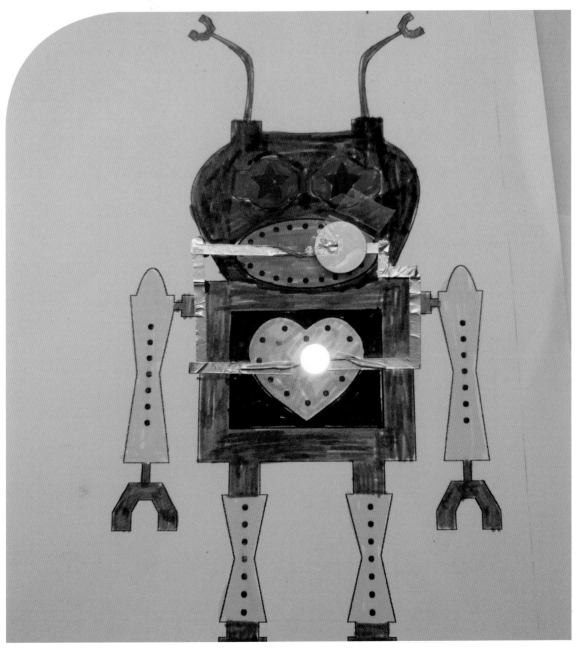

CHERRY LAKE PUBLISHING • ANN ARBOR, MICHIGAN

by Pamela Williams

CHERRY
LAKE
Publishing

A Note to Adults: Please review the instructions for the activities in this book before allowing children to do them. Be sure to help them with any activities you do not think they can safely complete on their own.

A Note to Kids: Be sure to ask an adult for help with these activities when you need it. Always put your safety first!

Published in the United States of America by Cherry Lake Publishing
Ann Arbor, Michigan
www.cherrylakepublishing.com

Series Editor: Kristin Fontichiaro
Photo Credits: Cover and page 1, ©Sandra Roberts of Kaleidoscope Enrichment, LLC / www.enrichscience.com; pages 4 and 5, Pixabay/Public Domain; pages 7 and 8, ©Michigan Makers/Regents of the University of Michigan; pages 10 and 13, Kristin Fontichiaro; pages 15 and 26, The Noun Project; pages 16, 19, 20, 22, 24, 27, and 28, Pam Williams

Library of Congress Cataloging-in-Publication Data
Names: Williams, Pamela, 1965– author.
Title: Paper circuits / by Pamela Williams.
Other titles: 21st century skills innovation library. Makers as innovators.
Description: Ann Arbor, Michigan : Cherry Lake Publishing, [2017] | Series: 21st century skills innovation library | Series: Makers as innovators | Audience: Grades 4 to 6. | Includes bibliographical references and index.
Identifiers: LCCN 2016055215 | ISBN 9781634726870 (lib. bdg.) | ISBN 9781634727204 (pbk.) | ISBN 9781634727532 (pdf) | ISBN 9781634727860 (ebook)
Subjects: LCSH: Electricity—Juvenile literature. | Electric Circuits—Juvenile literature. | Paper work—Juvenile literature.
Classification: LCC TK148 .W538 2017 | DDC 621.319/2—dc23 LC record available at https://lccn.loc.gov/2016055215

Cherry Lake Publishing would like to acknowledge the work of the Partnership for 21st Century Learning. Please visit www.p21.org for more information.

Printed in the United States of America
Corporate Graphics

Contents

Chapter 1

What Are Circuits?

When you woke up this morning, was it dark outside? If so, you probably switched on a light. Maybe you leaned over to turn off your alarm clock or unplug your smartphone from its charger. Perhaps someone is listening to the radio or

You probably use electric lights every day. But do you know how they work?

We rely on electricity to power the many devices we use every day.

watching the morning news on TV as you head down to the kitchen for breakfast. Once you get there, you pop your instant oatmeal into the microwave. Within the first few moments of the day, your life has been impacted over and over again by electricity. Most days, we don't give electricity a second thought. That is, until the power goes out and we realize how much we miss it!

The products you buy rely on electrical **energy** to work. If they're not plugged in or powered by batteries, they won't work. Although it seems like magic, electricity is really invisible science at work.

A Long History

Even though electricity has been recognized since at least 2750 BCE, it has only been a few hundred years since people began to explore how it works and how we can harness its power for our practical use. We owe a lot to past scientists who have studied electricity so that we can heat our homes, light our rooms, and run appliances to make our lives easier.

You can see what happens when you zoom in on energy and look at the smaller-than-microscopic level.

Everything we see around us is made of **atoms**. Atoms have smaller pieces called **electrons**. In some atoms, electrons are loosely attached. These electrons can break away and jump to other atoms that are also loosely connected. When electrons move from one atom to another, they carry an electrical charge. This charge becomes electricity when the electrons travel in a steady **current**.

For electricity to flow in a current, it must have a path that the electrons can travel through. That path is in the shape of a circle, which is why we call it a **circuit**. Every item powered by an electrical outlet or a battery runs on a circuit. Energy travels from the power source, such as an outlet or a battery, along a path until it reaches the item it is going to power, such

When you play with Snap Circuits, electricity travels through the metal snaps, which are conductors of energy.

as a lightbulb or a radio. It then moves back along another path until it ends up back at the power source.

Now think about how you could make a circuit of your own. There are so many ways to make your own circuits. Toys like Snap Circuits or LittleBits contain **components** that snap together into circuits. Squishy Circuits uses activity dough to create circuits. But why not combine electricity with paper to make paper circuits? Paper circuits are fun projects that apply the concepts of electrical circuits to art. You can use paper

With Squishy Circuits, dough connects components together. The blue dough has salt and other ingredients that make it a conductor. The purple dough does not. It acts as an insulator.

circuits to add lights to greeting cards, pop-up books, and many other projects. All it takes is a few simple supplies.

In this book, we'll be making circuits using copper tape, paper, **LED** bulbs, and a small 3-volt coin cell battery. Keep reading to learn more about each of these components!

Chapter 2

Gathering Supplies

To create paper circuits, we'll need some supplies. In this chapter, we'll talk about what you'll need and why.

Copper Tape

Peel-and-stick copper tape connects the various components to one another. Copper is perfect for the job because it's a **conductor**. This means that it can conduct electricity, just as a train conductor helps people and trains get where they need to go. Electricity can easily flow through it. Copper tape is useful because it lies flat on paper projects.

In general, metals (like copper, aluminum, gold, and silver) are good conductors. Unfortunately, water, people, animals, and trees can also conduct electricity. This means that living things must always use caution when they are around electricity. (This is why there are

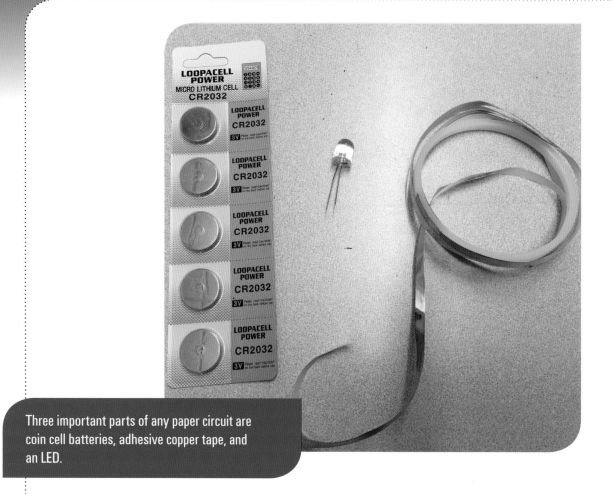

Three important parts of any paper circuit are coin cell batteries, adhesive copper tape, and an LED.

oversized stickers on hairdryers warning you to keep them away from bathwater!)

In this book, we'll use copper tape and the metal **leads** on LED bulbs as conductors. You can find copper tape in hardware or gardening stores (gardeners use it to repel slugs and snails), but it sometimes has so much adhesive on the bottom that only the top will conduct electricity. If you can buy double-sided copper tape from an online store like SparkFun.com or Adafruit.com, that's even better. Try to avoid using lots of small pieces of tape. You will get a better circuit with one long, continuous tape strip. When turning corners, use the folding method shown on page 16 instead of starting a new piece. This will allow you to keep a consistent connection in your paper circuit. If you must use smaller pieces, be sure to connect them securely. Use clear tape or electrical tape to secure pieces of copper tape together. Fold each piece at the end with the taped parts together and layer them on top of each other. This will ensure a good connection.

Paper

Paper is the backdrop for our creation. It won't interfere with the electrical circuit because it's not a conductor. It's an **insulator**, which means it will not conduct electricity. Other good insulators include porcelain (the material many plates and even toilets are made from), glass, rubber, and plastic. This is why wires are wrapped in rubber or plastic. It stops electricity from reaching your hands.

Getting Creative

Paper circuits are more than just electrical devices. They let you combine your science side with your inner artist. You'll make things that don't only work but are also a pleasure to look at. That's why you'll want to gather your art supplies in addition to your circuit-building ones. Think about markers, collage, colored pencils, watercolor or tempera paints, stickers, origami folds, and more!

Any kind of paper can be used for the projects in this book. Construction paper, copy paper, wrapping paper, and origami paper can all be fun to experiment with. Just don't use paper with foil backing on it. It can conduct electricity, and we definitely don't want that.

Paper is also easy to decorate with markers, colored pencils, or stickers. For your first projects, try using cardstock. It is a little thicker than normal paper, so it won't tear when you poke LEDs through it.

LEDs

LEDs (formally known as light-emitting diodes) will receive the energy and, when the circuit is working well, light up! The examples in this book are made with 5mm LEDs, which you can find at local hobby stores like RadioShack or online at places like SparkFun.com, Adafruit.com, or Taydaelectronics.com.

An LED has a negative (–) wire and a positive (+) lead. The positive lead is usually longer. How you attach the leads will affect whether it lights up or not. Be sure to attach the leads to matching ends of the battery. The positive lead on the LED should connect to the positive side of the battery. The negative lead should connect to the negative side of the battery. You can even buy a special kind of flat LED sticker from a company called Chibitronics. However, these are more expensive than regular LEDs.

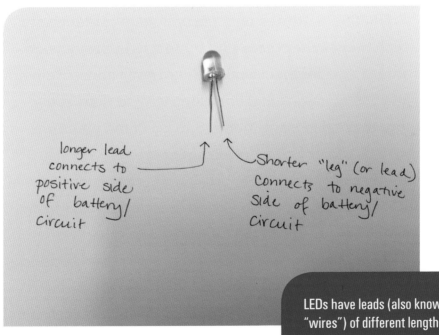

longer lead connects to positive side of battery/ circuit

Shorter "leg" (or lead) connects to negative side of battery/ circuit

LEDs have leads (also known as "legs" or "wires") of different lengths. The longer one attaches to the positive end of the circuit.

Coin Cell Batteries

Coin cell batteries are the best choice for paper circuits because they are flat. This makes it easy to attach them to paper. Like LEDs, they are clearly marked with two sides: positive (+) and negative (−). Pay attention to these labels, as they will play an important role in building your circuits. In this book, we use a battery size called CR2032, which is about the size and thickness of a quarter. You can find them at many stores. They are cheapest if you buy them in 2-packs at the dollar store or in bulk online.

CR2032 batteries only carry 3 volts of electricity, which makes them safe for you to use in projects. By comparison, an electrical outlet at your house delivers 120 volts of electricity! For electricity to flow freely, there must also be something to push the electrons along. A battery or a power outlet creates a force called an electromotive force (EMF) that does just that. Different amounts of power are needed for different inventions.

Be sure to store your batteries away from conductive material to avoid draining them. In fact, to avoid batteries touching one another and creating accidental circuits, it's best to leave them in the package until you begin creating your circuit.

Other Supplies

You will also need a few extra supplies to create the projects in this book. They include stiff paper clips or small binder clips (also known as bull clips), masking or clear tape, and markers or colored pencils.

Now that you know what electricity is, how it works, and what you need to collect to get started, let's make a circuit!

Created by VectorBakery from Noun Project

With this book, you'll be able to make a birthday card like this for a friend.

Chapter 3

Making Your First Paper Circuits

Let's get making! Let's start by making a simple circuit so you can see how the components work together. This circuit will use a piece of cardstock, one battery, some tape, and a single LED. The cardstock should measure about 5.5 inches (14 centimeters) by 8.5 inches (21.6 cm).

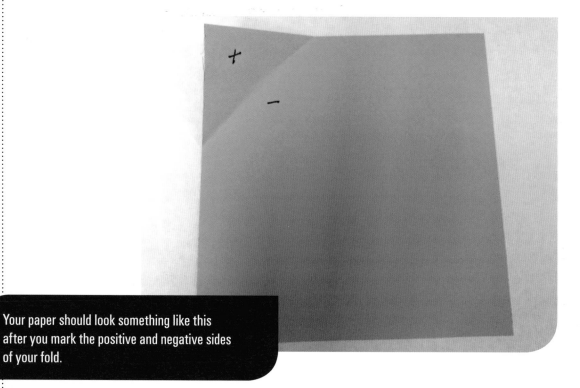

Your paper should look something like this after you mark the positive and negative sides of your fold.

Project 1: Simple Circuit

When we call something a simple circuit, we don't necessarily mean it's easy. All new projects take time to learn. A simple circuit is just a term for a circuit that has a small set number of parts and a simple design. The first thing we are going to do is create a switch. This is a way to turn our creation on and off by connecting or disconnecting the battery from the circuit. We'll do this by creating a flap in the top-left corner of our circuit. When the flap is lowered and touches the battery, the circuit will be powered up. When the flap is raised, the circle of energy will break and the LED will turn off.

To begin, place your coin cell battery in the upper-left corner of the cardstock. Fold the corner down just enough to cover the battery. Unfold the corner and make labels on the paper for the positive and negative sides of the battery as shown on page 16.

Open up the fold and remove the battery. Now unwind a long length of copper tape. Run it from the positive mark you made on the flap down to the bottom-left corner of your paper. When you get near the edge, don't cut the tape. (Whenever you cut the tape,

Positive and Negative

If your LED doesn't light up once you complete the circuit, the first thing you should do is check to make sure the positive and negative sides of the battery are connected correctly. In the example, notice that the copper tape connects the negative side of the battery to the negative side of the LED. The positive side of the battery is connected to the positive side of the LED. If you don't have the leads connected to the battery correctly, the LED will not light up.

you make it harder for the electricity to travel onto the new piece.) Just pinch the tape at an angle until it "turns" in the direction of your paper. Keep going along the bottom edge of your paper. Pinch it again when you get to the bottom-right corner of your paper so you can make the turn and head up the right side.

Now, you're going to move the tape up the right edge of the paper. You are going to make a break of about 1 inch (2.5 cm) somewhere along that right side. This will make space for you to add your LED. Then start a new piece of tape and keep going until you get back to where you made the (–) sign for the negative side of the battery.

We've kept our tape along the edges of your paper to make sure the paths don't overlap. Overlapping your tape could cause your circuit to short, or not work.

 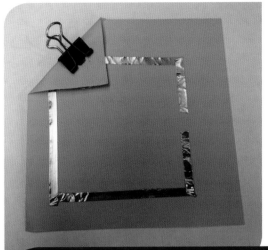

Use the binder clip to secure your battery in place.

Next, pick up your LED. Which lead is longer? That is the positive side of the LED. Use your finger to travel from the (+) mark you made for the positive side of the battery until the tape stops. Flatten your LED leads so it looks like your LED is doing splits. Use another piece of copper tape or a piece of clear plastic tape to attach the positive lead firmly on top of the copper tape.

Use the same tape to attach the negative LED lead to the other side.

Check your work. Are your connections firm and secure? If so, it's time to activate the switch! Fold down the corner flap. This attaches the copper tape from the flap to the battery, completing the circuit. Hold

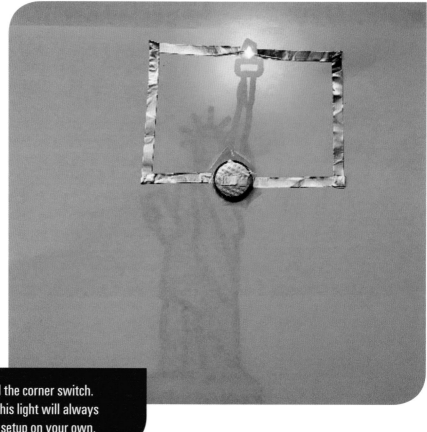

In this design, we skipped the corner switch. Instead, once connected, this light will always be on. Try duplicating this setup on your own.

the flap down with a strong paper clip or small binder clip.

If you constructed your circuit correctly, it should light up! If it doesn't, check your work against the picture again or check out the troubleshooting tips in chapter 4.

Project 2: Hiding Your Simple Circuit Underneath Your Art

Now that you have a sense of how a circuit works, let's make a paper circuit that shows the LED but hides the rest of the circuit on the back of the paper. Here, we will use a simple circuit to light up the torch on the Statue of Liberty. (We downloaded our image from TheNounProject.com, a great source for artwork you can use!)

Download or draw another picture. Decide which part of the picture you want to light up. Gently push both leads of the LED through from the front to the back.

Turn your paper over to the back side. Flatten out the LED leads. You might want to make a gentle pencil mark on the paper to remember which is the positive lead. Now visualize the rest of the circuit and sketch it out on the back side. Where will you put the battery and folded corner switch? Or will you tape the battery into the circuit without making a switch? (This type of circuit is shown in the photo on page 20.) Now follow your sketch and assemble and test your circuit.

What other artwork can you light up with a simple circuit?

Project 3: Adding More LEDs with a Series Circuit
Think about a project for which one light is not enough. Follow the instructions you used for Project #2, but instead of leaving one gap in your circuit

where the LED will go, try leaving three gaps for three lightbulbs. This is called a **series circuit**.

Try adding more LEDs to your series circuit. What happens? The more LEDs you add, the more power you will need to keep them glowing. If you add too many lights to a series circuit without adding more batteries, the lights will get dimmer.

Project 4: Adding More LEDs with a Parallel Circuit

Sometimes, multiple LEDs in a series can be hard to fit into your artwork. There is another method we can use, though. A **parallel** circuit allows the electrical current to flow from the power source and then branch

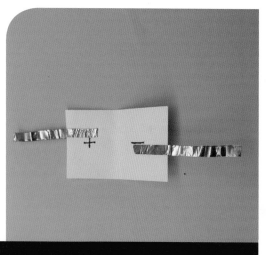

You can put a switch anywhere when you make a battery holder. See page 23 for instructions.

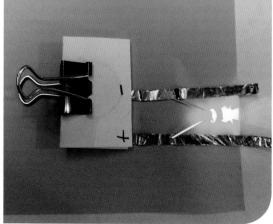

Making a Battery Holder

Some paper circuits are easier to connect when you create a little pocket for your battery instead of using the paper flap method. It's easy to make one. Just follow these steps:

Fold a small, rectangular piece of cardstock in half to cover the coin cell battery. Open up the cardstock and label positive and negative sides. Run copper tape from the positive side off the left end of the paper. Run another piece of tape from the negative side to the right end of the paper. Fold the cardstock closed again. Make sure the two pieces of tape hanging off the paper do not touch each other. If they do, adjust their positions.

Fold the end of each copper strip onto itself with the sticky sides together. This will ensure that you have good conductivity. Place your battery inside the folded cardstock. Be sure to match the positive and negative ends to the correct sides of the paper. Use a binder clip or stiff paper clip to secure everything in place. Finally, label the outside of the battery pack leads so you will know which way to connect it.

off into multiple LEDs before the energy comes back together and flows back to the battery. You'll need to make two long, parallel lines from your battery to your LEDs. (See the photo on page 24.) The positive ends of the LEDs are connected to the tape from the positive side of the battery. The negative sides of the LEDS are connected to the tape from the negative side of the battery.

To make a parallel circuit, make two lines with your copper tape. One should stretch out from the positive side of the battery and one from the negative side of the battery. Just like in earlier circuits, make sure that your lines do not touch or cross. You can place your LEDs anywhere on the tracks. Just connect the negative wire to the negative lead and the positive wire to the positive lead.

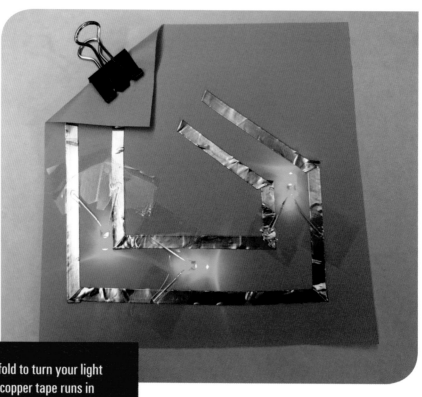

Simply open and close the fold to turn your light off and on. Notice how the copper tape runs in parallel lines and does not touch at the end.

Now try using a parallel circuit in a drawing. Hide the circuit on the back of the paper. Use a battery holder lead (see instructions on page 23) to light up your picture.

Add a bend in your copper tape to add more lights to other parts of your picture.

Project 5: Create a Switch Without Folding the Paper Corner

As you get to be a more experienced circuit builder, you might want to create things without folding down the corner of your paper. Remember that a switch is just a break in your circuit that can easily be reconnected or disconnected with a piece of conductive material. It doesn't have to be in a corner, and it doesn't have to involve a battery. Let's try it!

Make a simple circuit. This time, leave a gap somewhere in the path of the copper tape. This will be the spot for your switch. Place a strip of copper tape on a separate small piece of paper. Now set it on the missing section of your circuit. Make sure the tape on the small paper is touching both loose ends of the circuit. Your LED should light up. When the switch is

With a parallel circuit you can easily add multiple lights to a drawing. You can also use a series circuit to add multiple lights, but it can be harder to line them up closely to one another.

in place, tape one end of it to the paper that holds the circuit. Now lift up the side without tape to make the circuit open again. Your light will go out. Simply close the switch to turn it back on.

Chapter 4

Troubleshooting

Sometimes, creating with circuits can be frustrating. Things don't always work like you expect them to. But don't worry! This happens to even the most experienced **makers**. Finding problems with your creations and solving them is called troubleshooting. It is a big part of almost any type of project. If you are having problems getting your LED to light up, try checking the following things:

This circuit uses a battery holder (described on page 23). If your circuit doesn't light up, try checking the battery and LED connections first.

- Are the LED leads connected to the battery correctly? Reverse them to check.
- Is your battery placed in the holder correctly? Be sure you label your battery holder with + and – signs.
- Is your copper tape making contact with the battery? Open and shut your battery holder to check.
- Is your battery dead? Try it again with a new battery. (Tip: Disconnect your battery from your

Once you have mastered flat paper circuits, try using what you know to light up a dollhouse or model town.

paper circuit whenever you are not using it to preserve the life of your battery.)

- Do you have a complete circuit with no loose ends? Go back to the beginning of this book and make sure you made a closed circuit.
- Are the positive and negative copper tape lines crossing or touching each other?
- Sometimes, connections between components are not secure. Use your fingers to press on your LED connections to be sure they are making contact.
- Make sure that you are careful connecting pieces of foil. Remember that electricity will not travel through the tape's sticky side.
- Is the copper foil on your tape broken? Remove it and replace it with new tape.
- Is your LED burned out? Test another LED in the same circuit.

Now It's Your Turn

Now you have many strategies for making various types of circuits and switches. What else can you make into a paper circuit? Greeting cards? Pop-up books? Book reports? Electrified origami? Magazines? The possibilities are nearly endless!

Glossary

atoms (AT-uhmz) the tiniest parts of an element that have all the properties of that element

circuit (SIR-kit) a closed loop for electricity to travel through

components (kuhm-POH-nuhnts) individual electronic parts

conductor (kuhn-DUHK-tur) a substance that allows electricity to flow through it

current (KUR-uhnt) a flow of electricity through a cable or wire

electrons (i-LEK-trahnz) tiny particles that move around atoms

energy (EN-ur-jee) power from coal, electricity, or other sources that makes machines work and produces heat

insulator (IN-suh-lay-tur) a material that prevents electricity from flowing through it

leads (LEEDZ) connections between electrical devices

LED (EL EE DEE) an LED is a small bulb that lights up when electricity passes through it; LED stands for "light-emitting diode"

makers (MAY-kurz) creative people who make everything from artwork and useful objects to robots and computer programs

parallel (PAR-uh-lel) lines running alongside each other without ever touching

series circuit (SEE-rees SIR-kit) a circuit in which the energy travels into components such as LEDs in a sequence

Find Out More

BOOKS

Fontichiaro, Kristin, and AnnMarie Thomas. *Squishy Circuits*. Ann Arbor, MI: Cherry Lake Publishing, 2015.

Nelson, David Erik. *Soldering*. Ann Arbor, MI: Cherry Lake Publishing, 2015.

Toth-Chernin, Jan. *E-Textiles*. Ann Arbor, MI: Cherry Lake Publishing, 2014.

WEB SITES

Makerspaces
www.makerspaces.com/paper-circuits
Learn more about paper circuits and be inspired by other makers' creations.

SparkFun
www.sparkfun.com
This online store is a great place to buy electrical components for your paper circuit projects.

Index

About the Author

Pamela Williams is a teacher and librarian who enjoys learning by doing. She runs a Make-It Monday Club at her library where she loves to tinker and experiment with other makers.